CHESS
FOR PEOPLE
WHO CAN'T EVEN
PLAY CHECKERS

by Robert Danielsson

with drawings by
Mats Andersson

translated from the Swedish by
Thomas Teal

Adapted for the United States

MASON/CHARTER   NEW YORK · 1977

Original title: SCHACK FÖR BARN
© Text: Robert Danielsson 1976
Bild: Mats Andersson 1976
ISBN 91-7021-138-8 ..
Tofters tryckeri AB, Östervala 1976

Published by agreement with Lennart Sane Agency,
Malmö 25, Sweden

English translation copyright © 1977 by Mason/Charter
Publishers, Inc.

Published simultaneously in Canada by George J.
McLeod, Limited, Toronto

Library of Congress Cataloging in Publication Data

Danielsson, Robert.
    Chess for people who can't even play checkers.

    Translation of Schack för Barn.
    SUMMARY: Simple step-by-step instructions and
illustrations introduce the elements of chess.
    1. Chess. [1. Chess] I. Title.
GV1446.D3313 1977   794.1   77-21937
    ISBN 0-88405-559-0
    ISBN 0-88405-597-3 pbk.

FOREWORD

Chess is an ancient game. No one knows exactly when it was invented, but it was probably first played in India. Whether it spread to the rest of the world like wildfire or proceeded at a pace more in keeping with the stately measure of the game itself, chess has long been a truly international game—enjoyed by rank amateurs, good amateurs, experts and professionals.

But that still leaves a lot of people on the sidelines. Too many of those who have never played the game think of it as impossibly difficult to learn, and too many beginners are routed in confusion by the number of different pieces and the variations in moves. This book is based on a method for teaching chess to children that was developed by Björn Johansson and Göran Malmsten of Arboga, Sweden. (Chess is a wonderfully civilizing game for children—there are definite rules to be followed at all times, and players are forced both to pay attention and to respect their opponents, waiting after each turn for the other player to move a piece. Finally, it's practically impossible to cheat.)

The Swedish method presents the chess pieces one at a time and allows you to pick up a lot of what you need to know in easy stages. Meeting the characters in the world of chess, and getting to know what you can and cannot do with them, will make their ground familiar territory to you, and you'll more readily move around in it to form the strategies of play.

Since the concept of checkmate may be too abstruse for children, the object of the Swedish game is to capture the king and remove him from the board, which is exactly what would happen in regular chess if the game continued for one more move beyond checkmate. In their efforts to save the king, beginners gradually develop the checkmate concept for themselves.

To make it all even easier, the names of three of the chess pieces have been changed in this book so that the novice can better distinguish who's who among the

straight

diagonal

different chess pieces and associate various characteristics and powers with them. The pawn is called a *farmer;* the knight is called a *horse;* and the rook is called a *tower.*

Keep a chessboard nearby when reading—it will help you familiarize yourself with the real chess pieces and duplicate the moves shown in the illustrations. (If you still can't remember how the queen moves or in which direction the horse leaps, let your child read the book and give you lessons.)

forward

backward

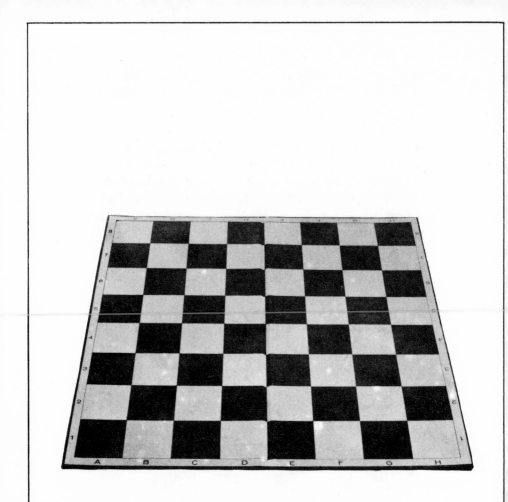

The chessboard, the battlefield on which the game is played, is made up of light and dark squares arranged in this pattern.

The squares may vary in hue from board to board, but they are always called white and black.

The chess pieces are divided into two armies—one white and the other black. These labels have nothing to do with good or bad—in chess, the good side is whichever one wins. The two armies are identical except for their colors.

White and black take turns moving—only one piece is allowed to move during a turn.

THE KING

Here is the white king, who is the most important chess piece (on *his* side, anyway).

Each side has a king; if he is captured, his army loses the game. More about that later.

Although he is of supreme significance, the king is a ponderous, slow-moving fellow. Perhaps he has gone in for too many royal vices.

The king can move only one square at a time.

The next time it is white's turn, the king can move one more square.

He moves slowly and carefully—that's how he got to be king.

And on his next turn after that, the king can move one more square.

He can move in any direction he wants to; it is a ruler's prerogative.

But only one square at a time.

Here is the white king and a black farmer (called a pawn in formal chess, he is discussed more fully later). The farmer has been rather careless and finds himself on a square abutting the one occupied by the enemy king.

The king takes advantage of peasant carelessness and captures him by moving to the farmer's square.

The farmer is now out of the game and must be removed from the chessboard.

Here, all of the king's possible moves are diagramed.

Remember: he can move in any direction he wants—
but only one square on each turn.

Here the white king and the black king are perilously close to one another.

It is white's turn to move. Any guesses about what will happen?

The white king captures, or "takes," the black king by moving to the black ruler's square.

This is a glorious moment for the white pieces, because, since they have captured the other army's king, they have now won the game.

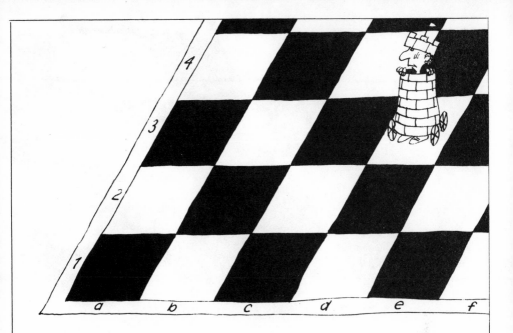

THE TOWER

Here is a white tower, who is called the rook when he is playing real chess.

The tower is a valuable chess piece because he can move as many squares as he wants—as long as no other piece gets in the way.

He has the choice of moving in several directions—but only one direction on each turn.

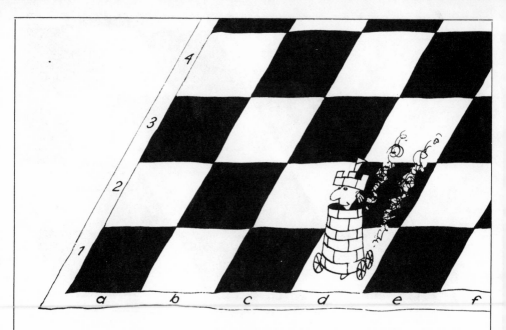

The tower moves in a straight line parallel to any one of the sides of the chessboard.

If the white tower wants to turn a corner, he has to stop first and wait until black has moved.

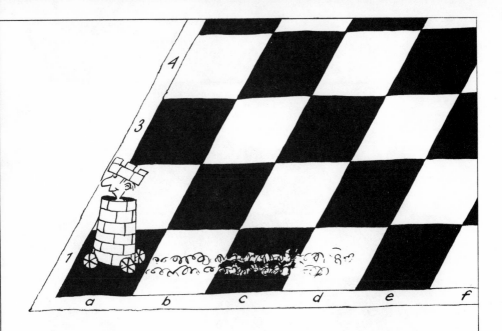

Then he can make a 90-degree turn and move in another direction.

Here we have a white tower and a black farmer. The farmer may feel secure because he is separated from the tower by an empty square.

So much for feeling secure. The tower moves right to the farmer's square and captures him. Having done that, the tower must stop.

The tower moves in a straight line—forward, backward, or sideways—but always parallel to one of the sides of the chessboard.

A black tower, a white farmer, and the white king are now on the board.

It is black's turn to move.

What can the tower do?

He can move straight toward the king, that's what, and capture the fellow—crown, scepter and all. The farmer is not too dumb to be distressed: the black army has won the game.

Here, a black tower, a black farmer, and the white king are all standing on the same row, or "rank," of squares. The black tower is a bit miffed: he can't capture the king because of the black farmer between them.

The tower can neither jump over nor go through his fellow chess piece.

He will have to go around him, and this will take several turns.

The king is quite amused, but if the tower has any say in the matter, the farmer will probably be peeling potatoes tonight.

THE FARMER

Here is a farmer, also known (formally) as a pawn. He is a sturdy, steady, but slow yeoman.

He can move only straight ahead on the board—and only one square at a time.

He cannot move backward, and he is not allowed to turn. He can only move straight ahead—and only one square at a time.

He is crafty, however, in the way he captures other pieces.

The farmer captures his opponents by moving ahead *diagonally* onto the enemy's square.

Here are two farmers: one is black, the other white. The black farmer is standing diagonally in front of the white one.

They are both on white squares, and, as you can see, squares of the same color are always connected *diagonally*.

That means one farmer will be able to capture the other.

It is white's turn to move. He wastes no time in moving diagonally to the black farmer's square and capturing him.

If it had been black's turn to move, he could have done the same thing to the white farmer.

The farmer, even when he's known as a pawn, moves forward one square at a time, and captures other pieces by moving diagonally.

FARMER'S CHESS

This is a game to play before learning real chess. It is played mainly with the farmers and without several other chess pieces you have not yet met.

In this game the towers are not played at the beginning. They stand at the edge of the board and wait patiently.

Here, it is white's turn to move. What piece can the white farmer capture?

Remember that farmers can only capture diagonally (on the same color).

Since the white farmer was standing on a black square, he was able to move diagonally to the black square his enemy was occupying and capture him.

Now it's black's turn to move.

The black farmer would like to take revenge on the white farmer, but he can't. He can only move one square straight ahead.

So it's white's turn again.

The white farmer moves one square straight ahead and lands on the last square, or eighth "rank," of the board.

This is an important achievement, and the white army is rewarded for the farmer's perseverance.

Because the farmer has reached the last square, he trades places with the tower, who has been waiting on the sidelines.

This gives the white army a significant advantage, because the tower can move farther and faster than the lowly farmer.

This is how the board looks when the pieces are set up for Farmer's Chess.

In this picture, we are looking at the chessboard from the side.

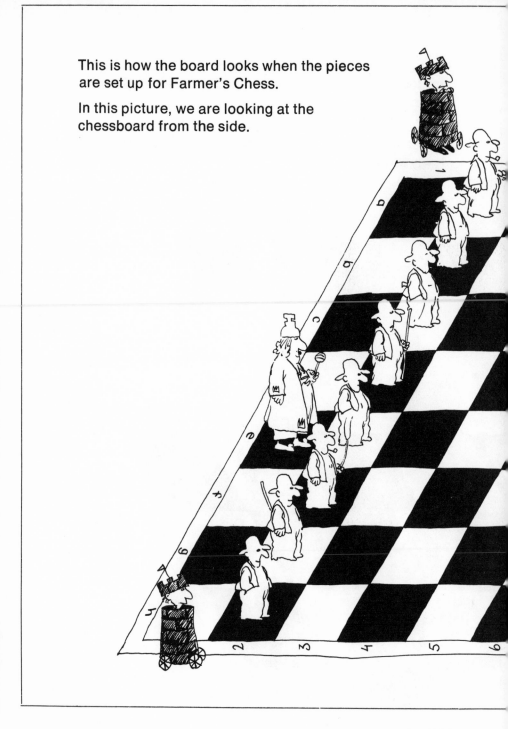

White always moves first.

On the opposite page you can see what the board looks like from the viewpoint of the person playing with the white army.

Notice that the white king always starts the game on the black square just to the right of the middle of the board. The black king is directly opposite him on the other side of the board.

The white towers are positioned just off the board on the black army's side. They will wait there until a white farmer has reached the last square. Then one of the towers will be substituted for the farmer.

The black towers near white's side of the board are waiting for a black farmer to reach his last square.

Before you begin placing the chess pieces, be sure that there is a white square in the lower right hand corner of your side of the board.

All is in readiness for the game to begin. You and the person you play against must decide who gets the white army and who gets the black.

Remember that white always moves first.

Play a few games of Farmer's Chess until you are familiar with the way the farmers, the towers, and the king move and capture other pieces.

THE BISHOP

Here is a new piece, a white bishop.

A stately fellow, the bishop moves diagonally. He always stays on the same color.

Like the tower, he can move as many squares as he wants—as long as no other piece gets in the way.

The bishop has the choice of moving in several directions—but only in one direction on each turn.

On white's next move, the bishop can turn and move in
a new direction.

Here are a white bishop, a black farmer, and a black tower.

It is white's turn to move.

Can the bishop capture either of the two black pieces?

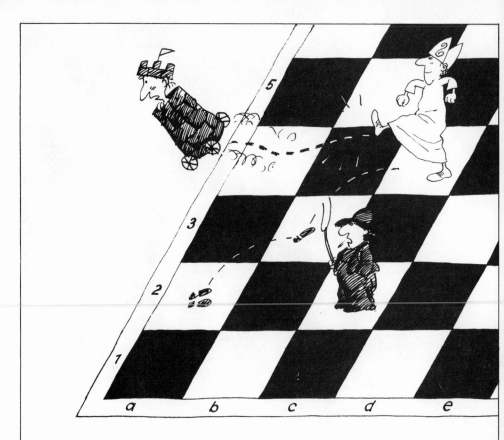

Yes. By moving diagonally, he can take the tower.

He could not have taken the farmer even if he'd wanted to.

Now we have a black bishop and the white king.

It is black's turn to move.

What does the bishop do?

He takes the king, of course—and the black army wins.

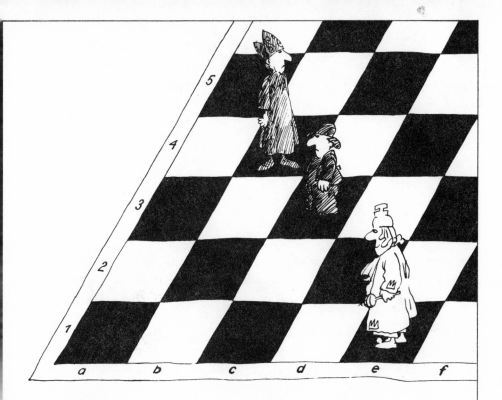

Here, a black bishop, a black farmer, and the white king are all lined up on the same diagonal.

The bishop cannot capture the white king because a black farmer stands in the way. The bishop probably would like to rid himself of the farmer, but he can't—they are in the same army.

The white king is safe.

The bishop moves diagonally on squares of the same color.

Set up your chessboard as shown in this picture. All the pieces are positioned the same way they were in Farmer's Chess; the only difference is that the bishops have now been added to the board.

Each side has two bishops, and they stand three squares in from the left and the right.

Play a few games using the bishops.

THE HORSE

The horse is officially known as the knight, but in most chess sets he really looks like a horse.

He gallops around like one, too.

The horse moves three squares at a time—two squares
straight ahead and one square to the side.

The horse is the only piece that can jump over others.

It doesn't matter whether they are black or white.

Here are a white horse and two black farmers.

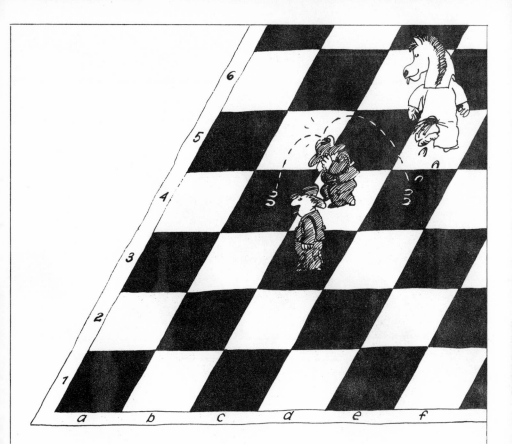

The horse leaps up—two squares forward and one to the side.

The farmer who is jumped over is not captured—he just has a headache.

Now we have a white horse and a black bishop.

The horse leaps two squares straight ahead and one square to the side...

and captures the startled bishop.

These are the possible moves that the horse can make.

A white horse, a black tower, and two black farmers.

It is white's turn.

What can the horse do?

He jumps two squares straight ahead and one to the side, and he captures the tower. The horse's leap has carried him over a black farmer and onto the surprised tower's square.

Now it is black's turn.

As you can see, one of the black farmers has moved ahead one square (diagonally) and taken the white horse.

Did you remember that a farmer always captures diagonally? The white horse didn't.

Now let's add the horses to the board.

Each side's two horses are positioned on the second square in from the left and right.

Play a game and see what it's like to make the horses leap.

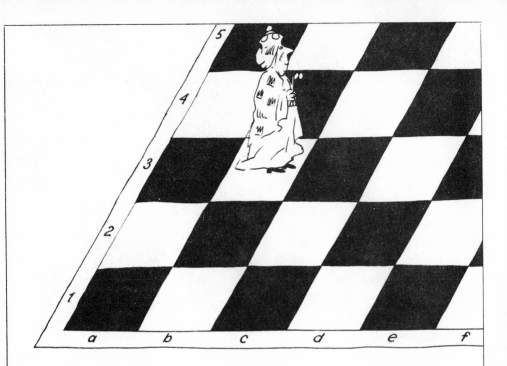

THE QUEEN

This is the white queen.

Unlike her consort, the king, she is able to move rapidly across the board. The queen's power and quickness more than make up for her husband's sluggishness.

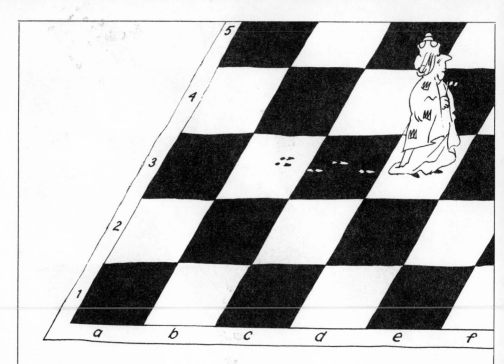

Like the tower, the queen can move in a straight line across, up, or down the board.

But only in one direction on each move.

She can go as far as she wants—as long as no other piece gets in the way.

The queen can also move diagonally, as the bishop does.

She is a power to be reckoned with.

All of the queen's possible moves are represented here.

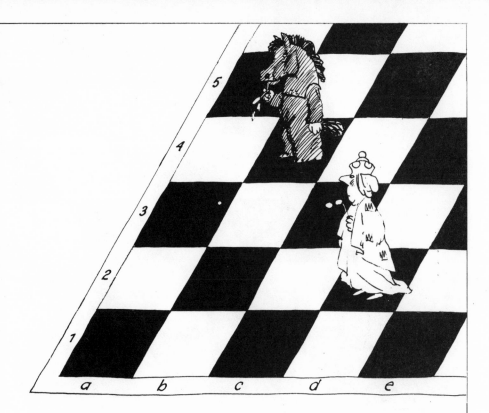

A white queen and a black horse—can she capture him?

Yes, in exactly the same way the bishop would.

Now we have the black queen, a white tower, and a white farmer.

Black's move—who will the queen capture?

She gives the farmer a royal bump off the board.

If you thought she could capture the tower, you mistook the queen for a horse. (Which was not very kind of you.)

Now the black queen, a black bishop, a white tower, and a white farmer.

In this example, the white pieces are safe from the queen. She cannot capture the tower. From the square she is standing on, only the horse could have done that (make no mistake this time).

The farmer is also safe because a black piece stands between him and the queen. The black queen cannot jump over or pass through a black chess piece (or a white one).

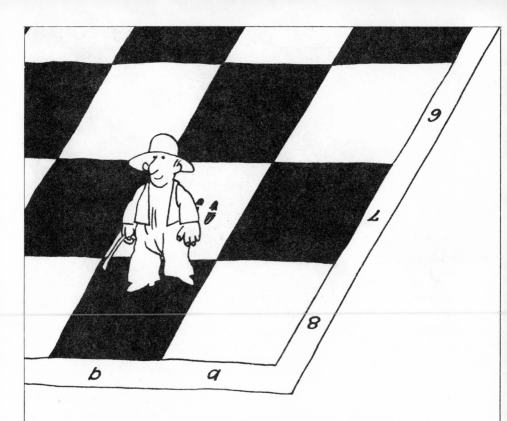

Now that you have been introduced to all the different chess pieces, we are going to modify one of the rules you have learned.

In the previous games you have played, a farmer who reached the last square of the board was exchanged for a tower waiting on the sidelines.

In real, formal chess, the farmer can be changed into any other chess piece you desire *(except the king)*. And there are no pieces waiting near the last square to exchange places with him.

Here's an example: you are looking at the board from black's side; the white farmer has just reached the last square.

The farmer is now changed into a more useful piece— usually it is best to make him a queen. If the queen with whom you began the game has already been captured and taken off the board, you can simply put her back in place of the farmer. If your queen is still alive and well, you will have to remember that the little farmer who reached the last square is now a queen also.

Each army starts the game with one queen but can acquire several more as farmers begin to reach the last square on the opposite side of the board.

Set up the chess pieces as you see in the picture above. This is how the board will look at the beginning of the game.

The queen will be standing on a square of her own color. The towers no longer stand outside the board. They are in the game and are positioned in the corners.

White always moves first.

Here are a few extra rules you should know as you leave Farmer's Chess behind and progress toward formal chess:

Each farmer is allowed the option of moving forward *one* or *two* squares on his first move. Remember, this choice is given to each farmer only on his first move in each game.

Players often start the game by moving the farmer who is in front of the king two squares forward.

In the version of chess you have been playing up until now, the winner has been the player whose chess piece captures the king by moving onto his square.

In formal chess, you win by putting the other player's king in *checkmate*. Checkmate means that you have moved a piece to a position attacking the king from which there is no escape for him.

In this case, how can the white tower put the black king in checkmate?

The tower moves up to the last row of the board. There is nothing the black army can do to save its king, so this is checkmate.

It is black's turn now, but since nothing can be done to help the king escape, black is not allowed to move at all. The game is over—white has won.

Here, the black tower has moved to a position from which it will be able to reach the white king on the tower's next move—unless the king can escape.

In this situation, the player who has the black army must say, "Check."

Saying "check" is simply a way of announcing that one of your chess pieces has moved to a place from which, on its *next* move, it will be able to reach the enemy king.

In this case, the king's response to the check is to move one square to the side and capture the threatening tower.

In formal chess you win when you have placed the other player's king in *checkmate:* on your turn you have moved a chess piece in such a way that the enemy king cannot escape *on your opponent's very next move.* Since the king cannot escape, your opponent does not move at all—you have won.

It is important to remember that a king is never allowed to put himself in check—that means he can never move to a square where he can be captured on his enemy's next move.

One more rule: the king can not move to a square that puts him next to the other king.

Now—you thought you only knew how to play checkers?